How God Takes Our Little and Makes It Much

How God Takes Our Little and Makes It Much

James W. Moore

Abingdon Press
NASHVILLE

HOW GOD TAKES OUR LITTLE AND MAKES IT MUCH

Library of Congress Cataloging-in-Publication Data

Moore, James W. (James Wendell), 1938-
How God takes our little and makes it much / James W. Moore.
p. cm.
Life application topics taken from The Wesley study Bible.
ISBN 978-1-4267-0878-7 (binding : book-pbk./trade pbk. : alk. paper) 1. Bible—Criticism, interpretation, etc. 2. United Methodist Church (U.S.)—Doctrines. I. Bible. English. New Revised Standard. 2009. II. Title.
BS511.3.M66 2010
248.4—dc22

2010001266

10 11 12 13 14 15 16 17 18 19 — 10 9 8 7 6 5 4 3 2

MANUFACTURED IN THE UNITED STATES OF AMERICA

For June

CONTENTS

1. God Takes a Reluctant Shepherd and Makes a Bold Leader: *The Story of Moses* 9

2. God Takes a Harem Girl and Makes a Heroine: *The Story of Esther* 21

3. God Finds the Lost and Celebrates with Joy: *The Lost Sheep, the Lost Coin, and the Lost Son* ... 33

4. God Takes a Fisherman and Makes a Disciple for All People: *The Story of Peter* 47

5. God Takes Our Little and Makes It Much: *The Story of the Church* 59

6. God Takes Mere Sinners and Makes Us *More* than Conquerors 73

Session One

God Takes a Reluctant Shepherd and Makes a Bold Leader

The Story of Moses

Exodus 3:1-20

Their names are Bob and Karen. They recently moved into a brand-new home in north Dallas. Bob and Karen are the proud parents of two fine boys, David (age four) and Jack (age two), and they were delighted to discover that all around them in their new neighborhood are young couples who also have preschool-age children.

Recently, two little girls from across the street came over to play with David and Jack. The two little boys were excited because the two little girls are really cute. Four-year-old David was especially pleased because he has something of a crush on the five-year-old girl. As soon as they arrived, all four children ran upstairs to play in the playroom.

Bob said they were playing together so well—no crying, no fussing, no squabbling—and no crashes. However, after about thirty minutes, Bob thought that he had better go up to check on them. When Bob walked into the playroom, David took one look at him and said, "Daddy, don't you have a meeting downstairs with Momma?"

That sounds like something a junior high or senior high young person might say, doesn't it? But it is also similar to what happened when Moses experienced the presence of God in that burning bush. Things were going well for Moses. He didn't want to be bothered or interrupted, so in effect he said to God: "Lord, don't you have a meeting somewhere with somebody else? Surely you don't want me to be the one to go face the pharaoh and demand the release of your people. Things are going great for me. Couldn't you call on somebody else?"

This was a dangerous mission, risky business, a frightening task that God wanted to lay on Moses—and Moses knew it. I mean, you don't tell Egyptian kings what to do. I mean, you don't tell pharaohs anything, do you? Pharaohs do the telling, and everybody jumps to quickly obey—or else! Heads will roll! Notice how Moses responds, just as we would have: "Who? Me? Lord, you're not talking to me, are you? Of all people... why me? You have got to be kidding. I have lots of good excuses. I'm not a good speaker. I'm not eloquent. And besides, I'm already in big trouble back there. And it's so peaceful here, so calm and serene. Lord, couldn't you pick someone else? I can't do this. Lord, I can't do this! Couldn't you go meet with somebody else about this?"

But God would not be put off. "Go, Moses," he said,

"Set my people free. Go, and I will go with you!" Moses, still not too excited about taking on the power of Pharaoh, hedges a little more, "But Lord, by what authority? I don't have any authority. I can't just go over there and demand the release of these captives. They are going to want to know where I'm coming from and by what authority I'm speaking from. Lord, who are you? Who shall I say sent me? What is your name?" God answers, "I am who I am." At least, that's the way most scholars translate it.

However, the great Old Testament scholar, Martin Buber, said something about this toward the end of his life that touched my heart greatly. After studying the original Hebrew text for many years, Martin Buber said he finally came to the conclusion that we may have mistranslated that verse. Instead of being translated that the name of God is "I am who I am," Buber believed it should read, "*I Shall Be There.*"

Isn't that beautiful? The name of God is "I Shall Be There"! That is God's name, and that is God's greatest promise, and that is good news. We can wrap our arms around that promise and always remember that whatever we have to deal with in this life, come what may, the name of God is "I Shall Be There."

Let me show you what I mean with three thoughts that emerge from this story of Moses in the book of Exodus.

I. First of All, When We Have to Face the Pharoahs of Life, We Can Remember That the Name of God Is: "I Shall Be There"

Can you just imagine how Moses must have felt as he approached the pharaoh? The pharaoh had all the power, all the clout. This was a scary, frightening situation that Moses had to face. He had to confront and challenge one of the most powerful, threatening, intimidating men in the world of that time. All of us who live in this world sometimes have to face frightening situations like that, although perhaps not so dramatically.

Let me ask you something. What are the pharaohs you are facing right now? What are the frightening, scary things you are up against right now? Is it a problem at work or at home? Is it a health problem? Or a financial concern?

Do you remember Dean de Ovies' famous cemetery story? When Dean de Ovies was a little boy in England, he used to play in the cemetery at night. One night he accidentally fell into a newly dug grave that was so deep he could not get out no matter how hard he tried. Finally, in exhaustion, he sat down in the dark corner of the grave to wait until morning. Suddenly he heard footsteps, then whistling (that's what people do in graveyards at night. They whistle!). It was his friend Charlie. Dean de Ovies said his first reaction was to call out for help, but he decided to wait a while and see what would happen.

Sure enough, Charlie fell into the same grave. Dean de Ovies sat quietly and undetected in the dark corner as Charlie tried frantically to get out. After a bit, Dean de Ovies decided to have some fun and he said loudly in a deep voice, "You can jump all you want to, Charlie, but you'll never get out of here!" But Charlie did! In a single bound, he went up and out of that grave as if he had wings!

Now, there is a strong point here, namely, the power of motivation. If Charlie were that motivated by fear, why can't we turn the coin over and be that strongly motivated by confidence—the confidence that comes from claiming God's most significant promise, "I Shall Be There"?

The claiming of that promise turned Simon the denier into Peter the Rock. It turned Saul the persecutor into Paul the missionary. It turned the weak, stammering, reluctant Moses into the powerful, eloquent, courageous Moses, the champion of Israel.

Now, we can claim that promise too. Today! Right now! In your life and mine, we can claim that promise. When we feel frightened or threatened or scared or inadequate; when we feel insecure or troubled or burdened or challenged by the frightening pharaohs of this world, then we, like Moses, can remember with confidence that God's name is "I Shall Be There"!

This is the good news of the Bible. On page after page of the Scriptures, over and over again, we find it— God's greatest promise—that he will never desert us. He will always be there for us. Nothing can separate us from God and his love. Whatever frightening situation we have to face, we can remember with confidence that God's name is "I Shall Be There!"

That's number one—when we have to face the frightening pharaohs of life, we can remember that the name of God is "I Shall Be There"!

II. Second, When We Have to Wander in the Wilderness, We Can Remember That the Name of God Is "I Shall Be There"!

Some years ago, a young actress named Jeannette Clift George had a wonderful dream. She wanted to take Christian theater into the marketplace. She wanted to put on plays out in the community to teach people the Christian faith, to reach people with the good news of Jesus Christ, to present good theater to the secular world that lifted up faith and family values, and that acted out onstage the drama of redemption.

But she was wandering in the wilderness. She had no resources, no money, no theater—just a handful of young, starving actors who wanted to be a part of her dream. On faith, Jeanette and her players started rehearsing a play. A reporter came out to do a story on them and he asked, "What's the name of your group?" Jeanette hadn't even thought of a name, but as she looked into the hungry faces of her fellow actors, she suddenly blurted out, "We are the After Dinner Players!" She said she thought, "We are all starving actors, so maybe with that name, somebody might invite us to perform after dinner and they might give us a meal as a part of the deal."

Well, that's exactly what happened. Jeanette and her company of actors would go to big banquets in town and get a meal, and then be the entertainment after dinner. Along the way their name was shortened to the A.D. Players—and you know what *A.D.* means, don't you? It means "the year of our Lord." Today, they have their own theater (they call it, appropriately, Grace Theater), and they are "the year of our Lord" Players, the A.D. Players, which Jeanette says is the name God had in mind for them from the very beginning. Today, Jeanette says we were "wandering in the wilderness, somewhat lost, but God was there with us all along."

All God asks is for us to be faithful to the dream, to not lose heart, and he in his own good time will bring us to the promised land! So, when we have to face the pharaohs of life and when we have to wander in the wilderness, we can remember with confidence that God's name is "I Shall Be There"!

III. Third and Finally, When We Have to Face Death, Then Too (Even Then, Especially Then) We Can Remember That the Name of God Is "I Shall Be There"

Let me ask you something: Did you realize that Moses never made it to the promised land? He died just before they got there.

- He led the people out of Egyptian bondage
- He led them through the Red Sea
- He led them through the wilderness
- He taught them how to be God's people

But when they came to a mountain where they could look over and see the land, Moses realized that his body was old and weak and worn, and that he didn't have the strength to go on. So he passed the torch to Joshua and he let Joshua lead the people on into the land while Moses stayed behind on the mountain alone.

Can you imagine how it felt for him to be so near, but yet so far; so close to the land he had dreamed of entering, and yet too old and too sick and too tired to go on. I can just imagine this conversation between Moses and God. I can hear Moses saying, "Lord, I know your plan is best, but I can't help but feel disappointed. I wanted so much to lead the people into the land. I had dreamed of that. I wanted that so badly, and now this. I'm so weak, so frail, so tired. If only I could have had a little more time."

And God answers, "Moses, Moses, you have served me well. You have done your part. It will very soon be time for you to come and live with me." Moses looks down from the mountain and he sees the people moving forward toward the land without him and suddenly Moses feels so alone. Moses looks up into the heavens and quietly he says, "Are you with me, Lord? Are you with me?" And the answer comes back, "Of course I am, Moses. Of course I am."

This is the good news of our faith—when we have to face the frightening pharaohs of life, when we have to wander in the wilderness, and when we have to face death, we can remember with confidence that the name of God is "I Shall Be There"!

A Biblical Perspective

The story of Moses' encounter with Yahweh in the burning bush is perhaps one of the most dynamic experiences in the Bible. It is nothing less than God's self-revelation. Although no one really knows for sure, scholars believe that God's name, Yahweh, is a play on the phrase "I Am Who I Am" or "I Will Be Who I Will Be." Only after this life-changing encounter with the living God did Moses return to Egypt to face his past and bring the children of Israel out of bondage. God replaced Moses' fear and made him a bold leader.

The Hebrew people, now freed from slavery, heard the same pun when Moses interceded on their behalf for forgiveness. In their desire to see their god, they built a golden calf to worship. We can easily imagine their fear about the future. But God reiterated the promise of his presence by telling Moses: "I will make all my goodness pass before you, and will proclaim before you the name, 'The LORD'; and I will be gracious to whom I will be gracious, and will show mercy on whom I will show mercy" (Exodus 33:19).

God's promise to Moses, and by extension to us, is a profound assurance of God's abiding presence. In essence, God says, wherever you are, "I Shall Be There," to use noted theologian Martin Buber's phrase. But though this burning bush passage might be familiar and distinctive, it is hardly the only time God promises to be present with his people.

Long before Moses appeared on the scene, God was busy with Abraham and his descendants. Consider Abraham's grandson Jacob. A heel-grabber right from the womb, Jacob lied and cheated his way through life, finally stealing his only brother's rightful birthright. Jacob left home with Isaac's stolen blessing and arrived at a place called Bethel. There he rested his head on a stone and had a dream. In the dream, God came to assure Jacob of his place in God's promise to Abraham and to declare God's continued presence: "I am the LORD, the God of Abraham your father and the God of Isaac.... Know that I am with you and will keep you wherever you go, and will bring you back to this land; for I will not leave you until I have done what I have promised you" (Genesis 28:13, 15).

Afraid, like Moses, Jacob was assured by God that God would be there for him. In fact, when Jacob returned to Bethel years later, he built an altar to acknowledge "the God who answered me in the day of my distress and has been with me wherever I have gone" (Genesis 35:3).

After the death of Moses, we find Joshua, Moses' right-hand man, faced with the daunting task of actually crossing over into the promised land and facing their enemies, the Canaanites. But again, God was quick to reconfirm the promise: "As I was with Moses," comes God's voice, "so I will be with you.... Be strong and courageous; do not be frightened or dismayed, for the LORD your God is with you wherever you go" (Joshua 1:5, 9). And with that assurance, Joshua and the covenant community of Israel walked through the parted waters of the river Jordan, this time with the ark of the covenant, and took up residence in their new homeland.

However, arriving in a land flowing with milk and honey was by no means the end of Israel's struggle. Israel still needed to be reminded that the God who called Abraham out of Ur, who met Jacob in a dream at Bethel, and who spoke to Moses from the fiery bush was still on their side. As the book of Judges showcases, Israel tended toward covenant amnesia not long after Joshua's death.

A couple of generations later, as the Bible puts it, "the Israelites did what was evil in the sight of the LORD and worshiped the Baals; and they abandoned the LORD, the God of their ancestors, who had brought them out of the land of Egypt" (Judges 2:11-12). The consequence of Israel's infidelity was to fall victim to the territorial aggression of their pagan neighbors. As a temporary buffer, God "raised up judges, who delivered them out of the power of those who plundered them" (Judges 2:16). One of those judges was Gideon, a fellow God found hunkered down in a winepress, threshing his grain. Gideon was afraid that his pagan neighbors, the

Midianites, would see him. The boldness of God's call of Gideon (spoken by an angel) is remarkably startling: "The LORD is with you, you mighty warrior" (Judges 6:12). Really? This guy hiding in a hole?

Again the scripture emphasizes God's promised presence to Gideon to help him overcome his fear. As if that weren't enough, the Bible's account of the call of Gideon portrays the scene almost comically. First, Gideon complained pitifully that the people's present plight was evidence of God's abandonment. Then he whined that he was a member of the weakest tribe and the least of his family and so could hardly be expected to help out his people. The cowardly Gideon also had a self-esteem problem, which God countered immediately: "But I will be with you, and you shall strike down the Midianites" (Judges 6:16). And Gideon did just that.

The Old Testament is rich with stories of individuals like Moses whose credentials were dubious and whose motivations were suspect, who were afraid and doubted themselves and at times even God. But over and over God addressed them as the "One Who Will Be There." The Psalms echo that promise over and over again. "I will be with you, says the Lord—"

That promise became a prayerful refrain for Israel at worship. Even today we read these words for comfort and assurance: "Even though I walk through the darkest valley, / I fear no evil; / for you are with me" (Psalm 23:4). From the prayer of worshipers, this promise becomes a cry of the prophet addressing a whole people in crisis—Israel in exile: "Do not fear, for I am with you, / do not be afraid, for I am your God" (Isaiah 41:10).

In the *Wesley Study Bible*, the notes that accompany Exodus 3:1–4:20 include this insight:

This encounter is powerful and dynamic as Moses meets the real presence of the God of Israel. Yet, the narrative is relational and conversational.... God remains resolute in his calling of Moses, but the dialogue displays patience with Moses. The implication is clear: the God of Israel is profoundly relational. (p. 70)

When Yahweh declared out of the burning bush, "I Am Who I Am," part of that self-disclosure was God's commitment to be present in relationship to those he calls. God can take our fears, anxieties, and worries and give us needed boldness and courage. Checkered pasts, pharaohs, Midianites, or Babylonians notwithstanding, God's word is: "I Shall Be There." Living fully within that promise makes all the difference and gives us purpose.

(See *Wesley Study Bible*, Life Application Topic: *Purpose*, p. 69.)

Session Two

God Takes a Harem Girl and Makes a Heroine

The Story of Esther

ESTHER 4:1-17

Standing Tall for What Is Right

I t was a Roman holiday in the fourth century A.D.
Eighty thousand people had come to the arena to
watch the gladiator games. The brutal gladiator
games were an accepted part of culture back then. Men
captured in war had to go into the middle of the arena
and fight to the death. They had to fight and kill one
another for the enjoyment and entertainment of the
people. Huge crowds would gather and roar with
bloodlust as the gladiators fought.

But this day in the fourth century A.D. was to be different from any other because in the crowd that day was
a holy man named Telemachus. When the gladiators

began to fight, Telemachus was horrified and appalled. He couldn't believe he was seeing this brutality and he couldn't stand it.

He felt that he had to do something, so he climbed over the barrier and dropped down into the arena. He then ran and positioned himself in between the two gladiators— and for a moment they stopped. At first the crowd laughed at the sight of this little holy man (still in hermit's rags because he had been living, fasting, and praying in the desert) standing there, refusing to move, standing in between these two powerful gladiator/warriors.

Soon the crowd became impatient and the chant from the crowd of 80,000 went up: "Kill him! Kill him!"

The emperor, wanting to please the crowd, gave the "thumbs down" signal. The gladiator's swords rose and flashed and before they came down, Telemachus prayed, "Father forgive them, they know not what they do." Then, down came the swords, and Telemachus, the holy man, fell dead.

Suddenly, the crowd was silent. Eighty thousand people there and you could have heard a pin drop. They were shocked by what had happened, ashamed that they had been part of it. They were stunned that this innocent holy man had been killed in such a brutal way.

Suddenly, there was a mass realization of how horrible and how wrong this killing was. And suddenly, in that embarrassed silence, way up in the top of the arena, one man, disgusted, stood up and walked out, followed by another and another and another until the arena was completely empty. The brutal gladiator games ended abruptly that day—and were never ever held again! (William Barclay, *Gospel of Mark, rev. ed.* [Philadelphia: Westminster Press, 1976], 203-5).

Telemachus, by dying, had ended the gladiator games forever. The spilling of his blood stopped the blood-spilling of others. He laid his life on the line in that moment—and his crucial action changed the course of history and saved the lives of thousands.

I can just imagine that as Telemachus entered the gates of heaven, his friends and relatives who had preceded him in death ran to him and said, "Telemachus, why did you do that? What were you thinking? Weren't you afraid?" And I can hear Telemachus answering, "I had to do it. Somebody had to do something to stop that horrible cruelty—and I was in a position to do it. Perhaps that was my calling. Perhaps that was my destiny, my purpose in life. Perhaps I was born for just such a time as this."

This powerful story out of history reminds me of the story of Esther. She, too, could say that: "Somebody had to do something. Somebody had to stand tall. Somebody had to save my people. It was my duty, my destiny. I was born and put in his place for just such a time as this."

Now Esther was more fortunate than Telemachus. She took her brave, courageous stand and survived. But she was determined to strike a blow for justice, knowing that it could cause her to lose her life. And that's why she is one of the great heroes of the Bible.

Remember the story with me. Amazingly, even though she was exiled in a foreign land, she had caught the eye and heart of King Ahasuerus, and remarkably, he had made her his queen. King Ahasuerus was a powerful man. He ruled over 127 provinces from India to Ethiopia. The people looked up to him, but they also feared his power. In fact, there was a law that no one could approach the king unless he called for them. To approach the king inappropriately was punishable by death.

The king had become disenchanted with Vashti, his former queen, and he had cast Vashti out, and then the king began looking for a new queen. Esther was a Jew and she was living in the home of her cousin, Mordecai (who was like her adopted father). Esther was brought from Mordecai's house to the king's palace and ultimately she was made the queen. Mordecai told her not to tell anyone that she was from a Jewish family.

Now, in this story, which is very much like an operetta, the villain emerges at this point. His name is Haman. Haman is placed in charge of all the king's officials. Haman gets caught up in his new power and commands that everyone should bow down to him. They all do, except Mordecai. Mordecai refuses to bow down to anyone but God. He will not violate the Ten Commandments. Haman is enraged, so he devises a plan to kill all of the Jews throughout the kingdom.

Mordecai notifies Queen Esther of Haman's devious plan and says that she must do something to stop this. And he tells her that this is her moment, her destiny, her calling, that she has been placed in her position for just such a time as this. Esther realizes that approaching the king could get her killed, but nevertheless, she does it. "If I perish, I perish," she says. "But somebody has to do something. Somebody has to take a stand. Somebody has to stop this killing. This is my moment. Come what may, I must do this."

Esther courageously takes her stand and through her act of bravery she saves her people, and thus becomes one of the respected and beloved heroes of the Bible. What a great story this is, the story of Esther.

Let's break this down a bit and see if we can discover those special things that made her life heroic. I put down three (there are many) and I'm sure you will think of others, but for now let's take a look at these three.

I. First of All, Esther Was Heroic because She Seized the Moment

In the hit Broadway musical *Stop the World, I Want to Get Off*, actor Anthony Newley played a kind of everyman character named Little Chap and he sang that powerful song, "Once in a Lifetime," which has these poignant words: "This is my moment, / My destiny calls me."

"This is my moment"—we have all known that feeling, haven't we? It's that special occasion when something stirs within us and we know that a unique opportunity is now available to us, maybe never to return again in just this way. We know the feeling of the crucial moment.

Sadly, however, we must confess that we also know the empty feeling of missing our moment, of letting the moment pass. Because of fear or timidity or insecurity, we let the moment slip by. We do nothing. We miss our moment and then we regret it greatly because we know deep down that we cannot replace it. That special moment is gone forever.

There is an interesting psychological point here. Psychologists tell us that every time we have this kind of feeling, if we do not act upon it, then we are less likely to act later when other such moments present themselves. That is, each time we fail to act, we become more closed, more hardened, more desensitized, more withdrawn, more emotionally paralyzed.

There is an interesting and colorful illustration of this in Native-American folklore. The Native American tribe called the Pimas believed that inside of them was a stone next to their heart. The stone had spikes sticking out of it. If they did something to hurt someone, or neglect someone, or break down a relationship, or shirk a responsibility, that stone next to the heart would start to turn slowly and the spikes would rub against the heart. The stone would continue to turn until the situation was set right or corrected. According to the Pima legend, the spikes did not cut or puncture the heart. They just rubbed and rubbed until the heart became more and more calloused. They believed the longer we wait to correct a situation, the more calloused we become.

How many letters have never been written? How many phone calls have never been made? How many compliments have been left unsaid? How many commitments are still not made because we missed our moment? The tragic people in history and the Bible were those who missed their unique moments. The great people in history and the Bible were those who seized the moment and acted with faith and courage.

United Theological Seminary printed a poster a few years ago that had these words:

The World's a Better Place Because
Michelangelo didn't say, "I don't do ceilings."
A German monk named Martin Luther didn't say, "I don't do doors."
An Oxford don named John Wesley didn't say, "I don't do fields."
Moses didn't say, "I don't do pharaohs."
Noah didn't say, "I don't do arks and animals."

Ruth didn't say, "I don't do mothers-in-law."
Mary didn't say, "I don't do virgin births."
Mary Magdalene didn't say, "I don't do feet."
Jesus didn't say, "I don't do crosses."

We could add to that. The world's a better place because Esther didn't say, "I don't want to get involved." Esther didn't say, "I can't take a chance; it's too risky." Esther didn't say, "Who, me?" She seized the moment, and thousands of lives were saved. That's number one— she seized the moment.

II. Second, Esther Was Heroic because She Expressed Sacrificial Love

One of the highlights of a conference I attend every year is the morning when the ministers who are retiring are brought forward with their spouses to be honored for their years of sacrificial love and service to God and the church. As the ministers make their retirement speeches to the conference, it is a touching and inspiring moment. Some are pensive, some are humorous, all are grateful.

Some years ago in the Texas Conference of The United Methodist Church, one of the women told about how her husband had proposed to her forty-five years earlier. He was in seminary at the time and she said when he asked her to marry him, she didn't say yes or no or "let me think about it." Instead she said, "I can't play the piano." He said, "Honey, you don't have to play the piano. All you have to do is love the people. Just love the people." "Well," she said, "I did marry him, and for forty-five years, I have loved the people with great joy." Then she smiled sweetly and said, "In those forty-five years, I have to tell you there were a few times, not many, but there were a few times when I wished I had learned to play the piano!"

Well, sometimes it is hard to love. Sometimes it is easier to just think of yourself and what you want and how to feather your own nest. But, if Esther had done that, if she had put herself first, her people would have been destroyed.

In the spirit of sacrificial love, she laid her life on the line. She was the queen and she could have lost everything, even her life, but she put her own selfish interests aside and did the loving thing. That's what heroes do. Esther was indeed one of the great heroes of the Bible because she seized the moment, and she expressed sacrificial love.

III. Third and Finally, Esther Was Heroic because She Stood Tall for Her Faith and Helped Other People

On June 11, 2004, millions of people all over the world were glued to their television sets, watching the memorial service for Ronald Reagan, the fortieth president of the United States. Presidents, statesmen, journalists, ministers, and family members reminisced about President Reagan. They recalled the incredible, historic things that happened during his time in the White House: the fall of the Iron Curtain, and the tumbling down of the Berlin Wall. They recalled his decency, his conviction, his kindness, his communication skills, his ability to make a decision and move on, and his love for our country.

And they recalled his great sense of humor, even in times of crisis. For example, after he had been shot by a would-be assassin, he said to his wife, Nancy, "Sorry, honey, I forgot to duck," and he said to the medical staff caring for him at the hospital, "I hope you are all Republicans."

The memorial service was most impressive, but the thing that touched me most was how his children talked about his faith and the fact that he lived out that faith by treating the parking lot attendant and the elevator operator with the same respect and thoughtfulness he gave to kings and presidents and ambassadors and senators.

Also in that memorial service, two different people talked about how moved they were that just moments after he had been shot, President Reagan prayed for the man who shot him before he prayed for himself. He thought of the other person before he thought of himself. Now, where did he learn that? You know, don't you? He learned that at church. He learned that from his Christian faith. He learned that from Jesus.

In similar fashion in this colorful Old Testament story of Queen Esther, when the king offered Esther anything, anything she asked for—even up to half of his kingdom—Esther never once thought of herself. She only thought of helping other people. And that's why Esther is one of the great heroes of the Bible—because she was born for just such a time as that and she courageously rose to the occasion. She seized the moment. She expressed sacrificial love. And she stood tall for her faith and helped other people.

A Biblical Perspective

With one of the Bible's most remarkable stories of heroism comes one of the Bible's more compelling

pronouncements of hope: "Who knows?" says Mordecai to Esther, "Perhaps you have come to royal dignity
for just such a time as this" (Esther 4:14). The message
underlying Mordecai's observation is clear—divine
providence has been at work in Esther's life all along so
that at the precise moment she can act—both on her
own behalf and on behalf of her people. The introduction to the book of Esther in the *Wesley Study Bible* puts
it this way:

> Although God is never mentioned, as Wesley notes,
> "the finger of God" directs events (Notes, Esther ¶1).
> Behind the events, with their dramatic plot reversals,
> stands not just divine order but also a divine ordering.
> The audience is meant to see that such divine ordering
> calls not for a fatalistic submission to some pre
> orchestrated plan, but for personal willingness to act
> faithfully in response to divine opportunities. (p. 601)

"Divine ordering" is an important phrase, one that
brings to mind Bible stories similar to Esther's. In fact,
biblical scholars point out that the first readers of the
story of Esther would likely have recalled the story of
Joseph. Remember him? The bratty son of Jacob who
ticked off his brothers and ended up sold into slavery?
Like Esther, Joseph found himself providentially placed
in the service of the royal court. At first, he was not connected directly to the palace of Egypt's reigning
pharaoh, but became a servant to Potiphar, the captain
of the guard. Nonetheless, "the LORD was with Joseph,
and he became a successful man" (Genesis 39:2).

As with Esther, Joseph found favor among his foreign
captors, initially with Potiphar, and ultimately with the
great Pharaoh himself. But along the way, Joseph's del-

icate situation as a successful outsider was threatened by someone from the royal court's inner circle: Potiphar's wife. You'll remember that the Bible describes Joseph as handsome and good-looking, a rare passage denoting someone's physical appearance. In the story, that quality is what set into motion a series of events that threatened Joseph and—keeping in mind what he will eventually accomplish for his family—Joseph's gracious acts on behalf of God's people. Potiphar's wife desired Joseph and attempted to use her position to seduce him. Joseph refused by appealing to his unwavering obedience to those who held him accountable (Genesis 39:8-9).

In the face of grave moral danger, Joseph took a stand, maintaining his trust in the boundaries set forth by his earthly master and in the tradition established by the God of Israel. His reward? He was falsely accused and sent to prison. Only when Pharaoh needs a dream interpreted and one of Joseph's cellmates remembered a promise, was Joseph restored to his position in the royal court. And this time he rose to even greater power than before (see Genesis 41:39-40).

It is from this position that Joseph—like Esther—could act on behalf of his people. Joseph predicted and prepared for the coming famine, provided food for his family, and finally reconciled with the brothers who meant him harm. Joseph was a hero—but one who recognized and informed his brothers of the true source of his heroism (see Genesis 45:4-8). The story of Joseph, like the story of Esther, is one of timing—God's providential timing.

To use Wesley's term again, it is "the finger of God" that touched the lives of Esther and Joseph and provided them with a time and place to make a choice. The substance of their heroism was that they affirmed God's sovereignty by their actions and, in the process, secured their success and a successful future for God's people.

(See *Wesley Study Bible*, Life Application Topic: *Success*, p. 607.)

Session Three

God Finds the Lost and Celebrates with Joy

The Lost Sheep, the Lost Coin, and the Lost Son

LUKE 15

Have you ever been lost? You have probably gotten lost somewhere at sometime in your life. It is a terrible feeling, and frightening. Panic sets in quickly; you start walking fast, your eyes darting in every direction, scanning the horizon, searching frantically for any familiar sign. Then you begin to run, in the desperate hope that running will somehow help you find your way more quickly. Time seems different when you are lost, and a scant few minutes of lostness feels like an eternity. Being lost is an awful experience!

I got lost at the world-famous Ringling Brothers' Circus performing at Ellis Auditorium in Memphis, Tennessee. There were more than twenty thousand people there that night. I was seven years old at the time. I felt sick deep down in the pit of my stomach. I was scared to death. I was all alone in that huge crowd at the concession stand. I didn't know which ramp to go up; I didn't know which section we were seated in. All the ramps and entrances looked the same to me all of a sudden. I couldn't find my ticket stub, and to top it off, I had lost my appetite for cotton candy. Terrified now, I did what most frightened seven-year-old boys would do: I went up the wrong ramp and when I got into the huge auditorium I turned the wrong way! Nothing looked familiar. The clowns weren't funny to me in that moment. I wondered if I would ever see my family again. I started to run, trying (not too successfully) to fight back the tears.

Panic-stricken, I looked frantically for a familiar sign or a friendly face, but no luck; all eyes were riveted on the clowns in the center circle of the arena. Everyone was laughing loudly at the antics of the clowns. I remember thinking, "How can they laugh at a time like this? How can they laugh so much when I feel so lost?" Just then, I felt a familiar touch on my shoulder. I turned around to be gathered up into strong, loving arms. It was my dad. My father had come after me and he had found me. It was a good thing he did, because I was running as fast as my tired, scared, legs would carry me—in the wrong direction. He held me for a moment, calmed me down, reassured me, and then took me downstairs and bought me a Coke, a hot dog, a yo-yo, a lizard, a little stuffed brown bear, and a candy apple. I learned a valuable lesson that day, namely, that getting lost is terrible but being found is wonderful!

Feeling lost is one of the worst feelings I know. And did you know that some people go through life feeling lost all the time? They feel out of touch, rejected, cut-off, estranged, alienated, out of place. And all of us feel lost like that some of the time! When we do, it is probably a red flag for us, a sign that we have lost our way with God. If we don't keep our relationship with God fresh, and if we don't renew our commitment to God every day, if we don't stay close to the church, if we don't spend some time in prayer, we can become lost so fast, it can make our heads spin! Jesus realized this, and in the Gospel of Luke he strings together three powerful parables that show vividly how people get lost and how they are found. In the three famous parables of the Lost Sheep, the Lost Coin, and the Lost Son, we see that there are several ways we can get lost.

I. We Can Get Lost by Wandering Off

We can get lost by unintentionally, carelessly wandering off like a lost sheep. I am sure that, in the parable, the little lamb did not mean to get lost; it was not his intention to separate himself from the rest of the flock and from the shepherd. He just began nibbling on some grass, and it was so good that he kept on nibbling with his head down until all of a sudden he looked up and the rest of the sheep were nowhere to be seen, and neither was the shepherd. Notice, they didn't run off and leave him. They didn't desert him or hide from him. He just wandered away when no one was looking. He didn't keep in touch! He didn't mean to get lost, but that's what happens when you wander off.

This can happen in our relationship with God. We can drift away, wander off, lose contact, and slide out of touch. We don't mean to slip away from God, but carelessly, unintentionally, sometimes we do. We don't pay enough attention to our relationship with God. We don't discipline ourselves to keep the relationship fresh and vibrant and alive, and then all of a sudden it has grown cold and we have gotten lost. Someone once defined religion as "friendship with God." I like that idea: faith is friendship with God! And we all know that friendships survive by association, by contact, by being in touch. The friends most real to you right now are those with whom you associate most. The friends most real to you right now are those you spend time with! Suppose some years ago that you had a friend who lived next door. You worked together for the same company; you saw him practically every day. You were neighbors doing favors for each other constantly. You enjoyed being together socially; you played golf together, went to church together and watched sports events together. You were together part of most every day, and you felt close to him. The influence of his life on yours was real and vivid. Your friend was an important part of your life. But then you moved away to another city.

At first, you kept in touch by mail and an occasional visit or a long-distance phone call. But as time went by, your time together became less and less. And now you associate very little and as a result you have organized your life, your time, and your energies around other things and other people. Now, you still count him as your friend, but the influence of his life on yours is simply not as marked or as powerful or as significant as it once was. The simple law of association says that if two people are to be real to each other, they must associate, they must spend time together! There is an old saying, "Absence makes the heart grow fonder," and I'm sure there is some truth in that, but there may be more truth in that other saying: "Out of sight, out of mind."

Of course, the spiritual application of this principle is obvious. If we want our friendship with God to be alive and well, it is crucial that we associate with God, stay close to God, spend time with God, keep in touch with God.

Let me ask you something. This past week, how much time have you spent with God? In the past week, how many minutes have you spent with God in prayer? How many minutes have you spent with God in the study of the scriptures? How much time have you spent with God working for him in the church, serving and loving him through the church with your heart, soul, mind, and strength? Like a little lamb, we can wander off and get lost.

II. We Can Be Led Astray by Others

Other people can cause us (by their influence) to be lost. That's what this second parable is about. The Lost Coin did not sprout wings and fly away. It did not lose itself. It was not responsible for its lostness. Someone else caused it. The woman lost the coin. It's as simple as that. This reminds us of how dramatically we influence each other.

There are people who can be either lost or found because of me and my influence, and because of you and your influence. What an awesome responsibility we have! On what side of the ledger is your influence coming down? Are you lighting candles so others can see and find their way? Or are you causing other people to stumble around in the darkness?

Some years ago, as I sat in SPAR Stadium in Shreveport watching our son Jeff play baseball, a nice-looking young man sat down beside me and struck up a conversation. He said: "Are you Jim Moore?" When I answered yes, he continued, "You're a minister, aren't you?" But before I could answer, he said, "You know, Jim, I've never been to a church service in my life." "Why not?" I asked. "Well," he said, "I had a bad experience with a church when I was twelve years old. My family didn't go to church, and I didn't know anything about it. But I was curious, so one Saturday afternoon, I went in this church building near my home to look around. I didn't mean any harm, but while I was in there, this man came up behind me and grabbed me, and accused me of trying to steal something. He ran me out and threatened to call the police. I've never been back in a church. I guess it's unfair to judge the church by that one experience, but to this day when I think of the church, I think of that man and the look on his face, and the tone of his voice, his hateful attitude, and I shudder. I cringe inside."

How vital it is that we in the church realize the importance of our influence on every single person we meet! At any given moment, our influence, our tone of voice, our touch, even the look on our face may turn them on to the church, or it may turn them away from the church. Some people get lost by wandering away; others get lost by being led astray by the influence of others.

Of course, the other side of the coin is that we have to be strong enough to take charge of our own lives, to know our own minds, to be obedient to our commitments so that bad influences or mixed-up people or peer pressures or current fads will not be able to pull us down or tear us away from our devotion to God and his church.

III. We Can Get Lost by Arrogantly Choosing to Run Away

Some people do indeed get lost by rebelling and running away from their responsibilities, by looking for love in all the wrong places, by looking for life in the "far country" of selfishness.

This was how the Prodigal Son got lost. He chose to go to the far country. He got restless and came to his father, saying that he wanted to leave home. "Give me my inheritance now. I don't want to wait around until you die. I want my money now. I don't want to answer to anyone. I want to be my own boss, and do my own thing."

When you look at this prodigal son, the descriptive adjectives fly fast and furious: rebellious, restless, discontented, presumptuous, ruthless, arrogant, prideful, immature, self-centered. But all these are symptoms of something deeper! What is his sin? What is his lostness? Simply this: even though he is a child, he doesn't want to be a child and even though he is a brother, he doesn't want to be a brother. He rejects his father and his brother, and anytime you do that, you are in the far country, because you are far from what God intended you to be. God meant us to be children to him, and brothers and sisters to one another. It's hard to remember that sometimes because we want to be number one.

One of my favorite stories is one Bishop Gerald Kennedy told some years ago about a young man proposing marriage to his girlfriend. He said to her, "I admit that I'm not wealthy like Jerome; I'm not as handsome as Jerome; I don't have a country estate or a yacht or a private plane like Jerome, but my darling, I love you." The girl answered, "I love you too, but tell me more about Jerome!"

Isn't that the way we go through life, crying, "What's in it for me?" Or, "Tell me more about Jerome."

This was the prodigal's problem, and that was precisely what got him lost. When you run away from the Father and desert your brother, you are lost, for you are in the far country of selfishness.

IV. We Can Get Lost in Resentment

This was the Elder Brother's problem. He stayed home, but he was just as lost because of the resentment that was eating him up inside. He doesn't seem lost at first glance. He is at home, surrounded by his family and many other people. He doesn't look lost, but he may well be the most lost of all.

When you survey him closely, the descriptive adjectives again fly fast and furious: resentful, judgmental, envious, jealous, hostile, bitter, angry, self-righteous. He hears the music coming joyously from the house and asks, "What's going on?" A servant answers, "Your brother has returned home and your father is so happy that he has killed the fatted calf and called for a great celebration." When the Elder Brother hears this, does he run to warmly welcome his lost brother home? No, not quite! He becomes angry, hurt, sullen, and he refuses to go in. The father comes out to encourage him to come on in and join the celebration, but he absolutely refuses. His bitter resentment cuts him off not only from his brother but also from his father, and his resentment causes him to miss the party!

Remember the context of the parable. Jesus is speaking to a group of people who are self-righteous "elder brothers" who were aggravated with him for celebrating life with the down-and-out poor people. That's what resentment does to us, and it's the worst kind of lostness there is. Some get lost by wandering off, drifting away like a lost sheep. Others get lost by the influence of others, by being led astray or pushed away. Still others get lost by willfully, rebelliously running away to the far country. And then some stay home but still are so very lost in their bitter resentment.

These wonderful parables in Luke 15 are not just about lostness. More important, they are about getting found, they are about a God who is like a loving parent who wants so much to seek us out and find us, who wants so much to bring us back into the fold, back from the dark places, back from the far country, and into the great celebration. Notice that each parable resounds with joy when what was lost is finally found. These parables underscore what I learned the hard way at the circus when I was seven years old: Being lost feels so awful, but being found by a loving parent is absolutely wonderful! There is no such thing as a little lost, but thankfully, there is such a thing as God's abundant love for us.

A Biblical Perspective

In chapter 15, Luke presents a common scenario in his gospel narrative; Jesus, capitalizing upon the social dynamic of shared meals, offers a vision of God's kingdom. Here Jesus is dining once again, but this time he is joined by an altogether different group. Scholars agree that the language in verse 2 indicates that Jesus may actually have been hosting the people at table with him. The key issue of the Pharisees is that of table fellowship. For Jesus fully to accept into *his* fellowship the likes of tax collectors and sinners was no small scandal. It was, in fact, a breach of orthodoxy in the religious community, an undermining of its moral righteousness. It was something that just wasn't done.

The term used for "sinners" in verse 2, for instance, does not describe merely the Pharisees' disapproval of some people's lifestyles; rather it identifies a group of people known by the community to have violated the Mosaic Law, to have failed to maintain ritual purity—a group who were excluded from worshiping in the synagogue. This group included shepherds, who were listed alongside tax collectors on the Pharisees' "most despised" list. Although King David had been a shepherd, those days were long past and shepherds were now at the bottom of the social ladder. So Jesus' first parable, told in response to criticism of his table manners, would have struck a raw nerve in the murmurers in the audience. Particularly offensive would have been the implied comparison Jesus makes between the seeking shepherd and the God of Israel.

Another intriguing aspect of the parable heard by those eating with Jesus lies in his portrayal of the shepherd's surprising behavior. Jesus described a shepherd whose love for the one lost sheep is so great that he is willing to leave the rest of the flock completely unattended on the hillside while he searches for the one.

And we do not know if he even bothered to put the other ninety-nine safely in the fold. If the shepherd had taken care of the others, the shepherd's behavior would have been perceived simply as common sense, rather than as the result of an irrational compassion.

Perhaps even more incredible than leaving an entire flock alone to search for the one is the shepherd's reaction upon finding the lost sheep. Bringing the sheep home on his shoulders, calling together his friends to celebrate, makes no earthly sense. It was just a sheep after all. Certainly neither the Pharisees looking over his shoulder nor the sinners reclining around the table would have missed the obvious ironic twist in Jesus' story at this point. Once again Jesus has listeners exactly where he wants them—completely off balance and ready for the punch line in verse 7. In it, Jesus addresses the grumbling criticisms the Pharisees expressed in verse 2. With a single sentence, Jesus proclaims two great themes of the gospel: the generous magnitude of God's grace and the relationship between righteousness and repentance. Jesus turns the tables, so to speak, on his listeners by reversing the positions of the Pharisees and scribes, on one hand, and the tax collectors and sinners, on the other. The one in whom God rejoices is the lost sinner, the one invited to the table with Jesus; the ninety-nine are the Pharisees who, though contentedly grazing in their self-righteousness, are not the recipients of any celebration on God's part.

According to the parable, the religiousness of the Pharisees had nothing to do with God's kingdom or with the repentance that calls for a heavenly party. Notice, however, that the Lost Sheep—and later, the Lost Coin—is not capable of any kind of repentance; the sheep is found because the shepherd was determined to find it, not because the sheep deserved to be found. Jesus makes a striking point with this parable. Repentance is not changing from sin to righteousness, but admitting lostness, admitting the need to be found by God's graceful love. Neither the lostness nor the repentance is in itself redemptive; it is God's desire for the sinner that is redemptive. While we were yet sinners, Christ died for us. This proves God's love for us.

The second parable Jesus tells is virtually identical in structure to the previous one. Luke uses parallel words and phrases to make clear the thematic connection between the two. In this case, one of ten silver coins or drachmas is lost; a search is undertaken until the coin is found; friends are called in to share in the joy of finding the lost object. The criticism of the Pharisees' words in verse 2 is again the occasion for the parable. The main character in the parable is once more determined to find what is lost: giving up is simply not an option.

Since ten drachmas amounted to about ten days' wages, the sum of the ten coins would not have been considered a great fortune, but for a poor family it was a considerable sum. Like the shepherd's bizarre behavior in the previous parable, the woman reacts as if she mislaid a large amount. Considering that the woman's efforts in searching her house involved sweeping a dirt floor by the dim light of a tiny oil lamp, Jesus' listeners would have considered her search for the lost coin as extraordinary as the shepherd's search for the lost sheep. In their minds, the likelihood of finding either was nil.

The need for repentance is once again eclipsed by the profound joy God reveals to those who respond to the unmerited invitation of grace. For if one's relationship with God is based on merit rather than mercy, then participation in the celebration of God's grace is essentially impossible. Fortunately, God is in the business of seeking the lost, the least, the last, the outcast, until they are found. God not only celebrates when the lost are found; God also invites those who want to be a part of the kingdom of heaven to share in this joy. If the Pharisees left the table that day grumbling even more, than surely the tax collectors and sinners must have been singing all the way home.

The questions Jesus raises for us in these parables are pointed. Will we confess our utter lostness before God and accept God's gracious search for us? Or will we seek God's approval of our self-righteousness? Can we risk being found by God in the reality of our unworthiness? Or do we continue looking at our lives as one long struggle for merit badges? Will we join God in rejoicing over the lost who are found? Or will we grumble when someone doesn't get what we think they deserve? The parables of Jesus in Luke 15 are reminders that God takes great delight in seeking the lost and the left out, not because of anything they deserve, but simply because they are worth finding. God shares that great joy with us when we are found. That is a lot to celebrate.

(See *Wesley Study Bible*, Life Application Topic: *Generosity*, p. 1416, and Wesley Core Term: *Repentance of Believers*, p. 1415.)

Session Four

God Takes a Fisherman and Makes a Disciple for All People

The Story of Peter

JOHN 21:1-19

Some years ago, The United Methodist Church developed a valuable new teaching tool in the form of a poster that they called *A Christian Guide for the Discussion of Secular Films*. It's very helpful and interesting. I've used it many times. It really works. For example, once I took a group of young people to see *Gone with the Wind*, and then together we used the guide to discuss what we had seen, felt, experienced, and learned from that movie. On another occasion, I used it with a couples' class to discuss the classic film *The Sound of Music*.

I have also used it with other movies like *A Beautiful Mind, Chocolat*, and *Chariots of Fire*; with plays like *Godspell, Jesus Christ Superstar*, and *Les Miserables*, and even

47

with TV programs like *Everybody Loves Raymond*, and I have found that it works well every time.

The guide is divided neatly into three sections which basically ask these three questions:

- What did we see physically?
- What did we feel emotionally?
- What did we learn spiritually?

Section 1 of the guide primes the pump of our thinking by simply helping us remember and say out loud what we saw. It raises questions like these:

- Which scene or setting do you recall most vividly?
- Which characters stand out in your mind?
- Which physical objects do you remember most strongly?

Section 2 encourages us to relive the emotions that are played out in the story. What feelings did we see in the characters? But even more, what did we feel personally as we experienced this drama? Did we feel happy, sad, or confused? Did we feel angry, uneasy, or inspired? Did we laugh nervously at any point? Did we feel challenged or encouraged?

Section 3 of the guide helps us draw Christian insights from the story with questions like these:

- Where was sin occurring in this story?
- Where did we see grace?
- Did we see the Christ-event here?
- Did we see death and resurrection; that is, did we see someone dying to an old, inauthentic way of

living and emerging into a new way of life, from "brokenness to wholeness"?
• And how does the life, death, and resurrection of Jesus Christ affect what we saw and felt in the story?

Recently it dawned on me that the approach of this *Christian Guide for Discussion of Secular Films* is also an excellent way to study and explore the dramatic stories of the Bible. A great way to unravel a biblical story— and get to the truth of God proclaimed in it—is simply to raise and grapple with these three questions:

• What are we seeing here physically?
• What are we feeling here emotionally?
• And what are we learning here about God?

An excellent case in point is the scripture lesson for this session in John 21, the resurrection appearance of Christ on the seashore, cooking breakfast for the disciples, and then having that poignant conversation with Simon Peter.

Now let me retell this story from the Gospel of John. As you read it, let me invite you to imagine that you are seeing it for the very first time as a movie or a play or a TV program. As you experience it, ask yourself these three questions:

• What am I seeing?
• What am I feeling?
• What am I learning here about the Christ-event and the Christian faith?

Look at the story with me. We begin with Simon out on his boat fishing and alongside the other disciples. He is brooding, thinking deep thoughts, not quite sure what to make of all that had happened. Then there is a flashback. He recalls how some months earlier he left his fishing nets at the seashore to become a follower of Jesus, and how Jesus liked him and included him and changed his name from Simon to Peter (Petros, the Rock) because Jesus felt that Simon was strong, stable, and solid like a rock. But then all of a sudden, things turned sour. Jesus was arrested and Peter the Rock got scared, and on that fateful night, he denied his Lord three times.

The next day, Good Friday, Jesus was nailed to a cross and Simon Peter was devastated, shattered, defeated, and brokenhearted. But then came Easter—and Simon Peter was at one and the same time thrilled beyond belief, excited, and gratified over Christ's resurrection—and yet confused and perplexed about his own future.

Peter returns to Galilee with his friends. Several days pass and nothing has happened. Here is where John 21 picks up. Simon Peter and his friends have been waiting there in Galilee for some time—just waiting, waiting for some direction from God, but nothing has happened. Finally, in typical fashion, Simon Peter gets impatient. He can't take it anymore, and he says, "I'm going fishing!" Now, it's as if Simon is saying, "I can't handle this any longer. This waiting is driving me up the wall. I'm worn out with the indecision, the waiting, the risk involved; and I'm going back to the old, secure life, the old life of being a fisherman." The others go along with him.

They fish all night, but no luck. But then, as dawn breaks, they see someone standing on shore. It's the risen Lord, but they don't recognize him at this point.

He tells them to cast their nets on the right side of the boat. They do and bring in a huge catch of fish, 153 large fish. John turns and says to Peter, "It is the Lord." Simon Peter, excitable and impulsive, dives in and swims to shore urgently. The others come in on the boat. As they come ashore, they see the risen Christ cooking breakfast for them over a charcoal fire. After he serves them breakfast, he takes Simon Peter off to the side and three times he asks him the same question: "Simon, do you love me?" "Oh yes, Lord," Simon answers. "You know that I love you." "Then, feed my sheep," the risen Lord says to him. "Feed my sheep."

Then the story ends exactly the way it started months before, with Christ saying to Simon at the seashore these words, "Follow me!" Isn't that a great story? It's jam-packed with the stuff of life—powerful symbols, strong emotions, and dramatic lessons. Let's sort them out with this basic, three-part formula.

I. First, What Do We See Here Physically?

What do we see happening here? Well, for one thing we see the disciples fishing, and this probably represents their temptation to give up, to throw in the towel, to go back to the old life. That's always the temptation of people of faith, isn't it? When times get tough, we are tempted to give up, to backslide, to go back to the old lifestyle.

Also, we see that it's nighttime—it's dark! Of course, they believed back then that nighttime was indeed the best time for fishing, but also this symbolizes their despair, their fear, and their confusion. At the dawning of a new day the risen Lord comes, or does the resurrected

Christ bring the dawn? The point is, until he appeared, they were still in the dark!

Notice also, the fishing nets overflowing with 153 different kinds of fish. What does that mean? What are we to make of this? Why the specific number 153? It's because at that time they believed that there was a total of 153 different kinds of fish in the sea. The number symbolizes the point that they are to be fishers of people, all of the people. That Christ came for all people. He is the Savior of the whole world.

The great catch of fish was gathered in the net, and the net held them all, and the net was not broken. Of course, the net stands for the church, and the message is obvious: There is room in the church for all kinds of people, people of all sorts, of every race and every nation.

Look next at the charcoal fire. English teachers would call this "foreshadowing"—a sign of things to come. I can just see the camera panning in on the fire. Remember that the flame is the dramatic symbol of Pentecost and the Holy Spirit. And obviously, the picture of Christ preparing and serving breakfast is a sign that this is a Holy Communion. "He was known to them once again in the breaking of bread."

And is it possible that Simon Peter's plunge into the sea represents baptism? As we look at all these things, all these physical things, it becomes clear that the major purpose of this story is to underscore the reality of the resurrection. The resurrection was not a vision, not a dream, not some hallucination, not a hoax. It was not the figment of someone's excited imagination, not a plot or ploy. It was not the appearance of a phantom or a ghost. No! The risen Lord has defeated death and is out there on the seashore cooking breakfast for his friends.

What we see here physically documents the reality of the resurrection. That brings us to the second question.

II. Second, What Do We Feel Here Emotionally?

This poignant story is charged with emotions: fear, guilt, remorse, excitement, self-doubt, bewilderment. Simon Peter is feeling all of those and much, much more. He is at the crossroads, raising the same question we ought to be dealing with right now: *How do I respond to Jesus?*

Simon Peter is facing the most crucial decision of his life. "Which will it be? Will I serve Christ or forget about him? Will I take up the torch of his ministry? Will I go on with it, knowing the great risks involved and knowing painfully that I've already failed miserably once? I wimped out, denied my Lord three times— three times! Count 'em! What if I do that again? Maybe I'm just a coward at heart. Maybe I should just go back to the old secure life on my fishing boat. How could he ever forgive me anyway? How could he ever trust me again? I bragged. I boasted about my strength and com- mitment, I talked big, but then when the crisis came, I let him down. I let him down."

That's what Simon Peter was feeling that day and that's why he was so quick to jump into the water and rush to the shore. He was always impetuous but there is more here in this scene. It was Peter's way of saying, "I'm so sorry I failed you, Lord! I want to be the first to shore, the first in your presence . . . because I'm so sorry I failed you."

Jesus was so perceptive. He knew what was going on deep down inside of Simon Peter, and just as he gave doubting Thomas what he needed by letting him touch his scars physically, now he reaches out to touch Simon Peter emotionally with the help and healing he needs. He takes him aside and says, "Simon, do you love me?" "Oh yes, Lord," Peter answers, "You know that I love you." "Then feed my sheep," Christ says to him.

They go through this ritual three times. "Simon, do you love me?" "Yes, Lord, you know I love you." "Then feed my sheep." Three times! Why? To let Simon Peter's threefold affirmation of love wipe out the bitter memory of his threefold denial. Jesus was saying to Simon Peter, "I believe in you. You are still the Rock. You can do it, but you have to put your failure behind you. You are forgiven. The slate is wiped clean. You can start over again."

That is precisely what the risen Christ does for us. He knows about our failures and our fears and he still loves us, he still believes in us, and he comes to us with healing and forgiveness. Physically, we see here the reality of the resurrection. Emotionally, we see here the beauty of God's amazing grace.

III. The Third and Final Question: What Do We Learn Here about God?

What do we learn here about our Christian faith? For one thing, as we have already seen, this story is about forgiveness. Can't you hear Simon Peter saying something like this to Thomas? "Thomas, you and I were both slow believers. Loving deeply, you were afraid to hope. You insisted on touching Jesus' scar, and the others sighed, wondering why you couldn't simply accept their words. But I know your struggle, those thoughts that beg for proof. But Thomas, like you, I've finally seen enough. I've never felt his scars. But he touched mine and with their healing, my heart cries with you, 'My Lord and my God.' "

This story is about forgiveness, and of course it's clear that this story is about resurrection. Christ conquers death, but he also resurrects us. He gives to us new life. That is the good news of Easter. And this story is about love—God's love for us—his gracious, sacrificial love for us, expressed so magnificently in the life, death, and resurrection of Jesus Christ.

But don't miss this. Christ says to Simon, "If you love me, then feed my sheep." The point is that the best way to love Christ is to love his sheep. He doesn't want burnt offerings or sacrifices or long, flowery verbose prayers, or painfully pious expressions—just love! Love is the authentic sign of discipleship. Love for others is the real symbol of our love for Christ. He wants us to follow him and imitate his loving ways. He wants us to understand that love is the most powerful thing in the world. He wants us to know that love makes all the difference. And God can take our little bit of love and help it grow to include all people. Just like God took a fisherman and made him a disciple for all of us.

A Biblical Perspective

The closing scene of the risen Jesus sharing breakfast with his disciples on the shore of the Sea of Galilee is so characteristic of John's Gospel: a simple event bursting with meaning. Throughout John's Gospel, Jesus' presence transforms even the most casual encounters—with a steward at a wedding, with a woman at a well, with two sisters at a graveside—into a proclamation of who Jesus is and what that means for the world, as well as for those who choose to believe in him. In other words, John's purpose in structuring his Gospel was primarily designed to disclose who Jesus is. Keeping that in mind, let us examine the occasions Jesus uses a simple meal to make a point.

In John 6, Jesus blesses five loaves and a few fish in the wilderness to feed a multitude of hungry folks who have gathered to hear him speak. And like chapter 21, where Jesus reclaims Peter, the whole of chapter 6 is a piece well-crafted to carefully convey a truth about Jesus and to encourage belief in him. The meaning of who Jesus is, is rooted in his sharing a simple meal with a group (in this case, a large group) of followers.

Notice, however, that the multitude Jesus encounters in John 6 has come looking for him not because they know who he is but because "they saw the signs that he was doing for the sick" (John 6:2). The people following Jesus are acutely aware of their own needs and understandably want Jesus to do something for them. It is important to see then that, according to John, Jesus "looked up and saw a large crowd coming toward him" (6:5), apparently anticipating their hunger. He knew more about them than they knew about him—or themselves (sounds like another group of would-be followers, does it not?). Jesus is ready for them. He is prepared to serve lunch to a hungry multitude on a hillside just as he will later be waiting to serve breakfast to the weary disciples by the seashore.

Like the needy crowd and the weary disciples, those of us who claim to be followers of Jesus may too often come seeking him for what he can do for us. Some of us may come looking for assurance that our earthly struggles can be conquered or mitigated, that our daily hungers—emotional or spiritual—can be met. Some of us may come looking for the right answers to our questions, for deliverance from what oppresses us, or for healing of what ails us. We crowd around Jesus expecting that miracle we heard someone else tell us about. We want a miracle for ourselves. Fortunately, John's Jesus is way ahead of us—he is prepared to offer us exactly what we need (spiritual bread) even though it may not be what we expect. That seems to be part of the message John wants us to understand in chapter 6.

Between Jesus breaking bread in chapter 6 and cooking fish in chapter 21, we read one other time when Jesus hosted a meal and took the opportunity to proclaim a profound message. In John 13, Jesus gathers with his disciples for a last Passover supper. It is another moment where Jesus seems fully prepared, this time to officiate something more than a prescribed ritual meal. Around this table, Jesus again offers himself, the Bread of Life—just as he did among the crowds and just as he will do after his resurrection—as the necessary sustenance for proper discipleship.

What is different about this meal, though, is that John's account of it focuses our attention not on the sharing of a meal but on Jesus' radical act of hospitality: his washing of the disciples' feet. What John most wants us to see this time is the towel around Jesus' waist. Jesus serves those he loves. Jesus also touches us at the point of our deepest need. Just as he humbly washed the feet of his followers, Jesus cleanses our dusty, careworn lives.

Recall that Peter's initial reluctance (probably expressing the tacit sentiments of the other disciples) was met with a sharp warning by Jesus: "Unless I wash you, you have no share with me" (John 13:8). Jesus' tone is similar to the one that accompanied his rebuke of some of the recently well-fed multitude in chapter 6: "Do not work for the food that perishes, but for the food that endures for eternal life" (6:27). Neither Peter nor the multitude fully comprehend what Jesus does or offers because they do not yet understand who he is. Peter does not yet recognize Jesus as a servant who will submit to suffering and sacrifice to bring in God's kingdom. The multitude who have eaten their fill from a basket of bread do not yet see Jesus as the One who will sustain their spiritual lives. They want Jesus to remain *their* personal miracle-worker. Similarly, Peter wants Jesus to remain *his* leader and master. "Be the master that I want you to be," Peter may think. Or perhaps he thinks, "Be the master that I secretly aspire to become, not some lowly slave just good for washing other people's feet."

Just like us. Which would you rather be, the teacher or the servant at the door? Where do you need to be for your own spiritual growth?

(See *Wesley Study Bible*, Life Application Topics: *Touch*, p. 1306; *Loving God*, p. 1310; *Jesus Died for You*, p. 1316; and *Doubt*, p. 1318.)

Session Five

God Takes Our Little and Makes It Much

The Story of the Church

ACTS 2:1-13

In his book, *Come Share the Being*, Bob Benson writes about God's incredible grace and the amazing ways in which God seeks us out and shares himself with us. He says:

> Do you remember when they had those old-fashioned Sunday School picnics? ... And when you got ready to pack your lunch, all you could find in the refrigerator was one dried-up piece of baloney? And when it came time to eat, you sat at the end of a table and spread out your sandwich. But, the folks next to you—the lady was a good cook and she had worked all day and she had fried chicken and baked beans and potato salad and home-made rolls and sliced tomatoes and pickles and olives and celery and topped it off with two big home-made chocolate pies. And they spread it all out beside you and there you were with your stale baloney

sandwich. But then they said to you, "Hey, why don't we put it all together?" And so you did, eating like a prince when you came like a pauper.

The point is obvious. We bring our little and God brings his much and in his grace he says, "Let's put it all together."

Have you heard the story about the young man who approached the father of his girlfriend one evening to ask his permission for them to marry? The father was skeptical. He said, "Son, I like you. I think you are a fine person, but I honestly don't think you know what you're asking for. My daughter is a wonderful girl, but she has very extravagant tastes. I doubt very much that you will ever be able to support her. I'm a wealthy man and I can barely manage it myself." The young man thought for a moment before he answered. "Sir, I think I have it," he said. "You and I could just pool our resources!"

Now, interestingly, both of these stories—the Sunday school picnic story and the story of the young man asking for his girlfriend's hand in marriage—remind me of one of the greatest stories in all the Bible, the story of Pentecost. The disciples felt empty-handed. They felt spiritually bankrupt. They felt inadequate and unprepared. They felt that they didn't have much to bring to the table or to the altar. But then God said: "Let's put it all together! Let's pool our resources! Bring what you have and I'll take care of the rest!"

I. The Story Reminds Us That the Holy Spirit United People and That We Should Live in That Inclusive Spirit

In the Old Testament story of the tower of Babel, the spirit of pride and arrogance and selfishness prevails. At the end of the story, the people are divided and separated and their languages are all mixed up. Here in the Pentecost story, the opposite takes place, the Holy Spirit of God prevails. Look at what happens: people of different nations and cultures and races are brought together. They communicate, they become as one, they are included and they are united. The point is clear. When we have the Holy Spirit in our hearts, we will be quick to welcome people with open arms and anxious to make the outsider feel like an insider.

Fred Craddock tells the story about a congregation he once served where that was not the case, where people didn't believe that way. This little church was out in the country. The area was experiencing a boom because of the start-up of the Atomic Energy Commission. Seemingly overnight, the village became a city. Suddenly there were tents and house trailers everywhere you looked. Construction workers began arriving from most every state in the union.

Fred Craddock's church was pretty small and just seated about eighty people. It had hand-carved pews and a little organ over in a corner that you had to pump. A beautiful little building—and very aristocratic! Dr. Craddock called his board together and told them what a great evangelistic opportunity they had, to reach out and evangelize all these thousands of folks who had recently moved in. He wanted to make them welcome and bring them into the church.

But the board chairman said: "No way!" "Why?" "They're not our kind." "What do you mean, they're not our kind?" And the board chairman said: "Well, they're just living in tents and trailers and everything. They're laborers. They follow construction. No roots.

They're not our kind! They wouldn't fit in!" Fred Craddock and the board chairman debated this back and forth and finally they called for a meeting after church the very next Sunday.

There was a motion immediately on the floor. "I move that anybody seeking membership in this church must own property in this county." "Second," someone said quickly. The board chairman reminded young Fred Craddock that since he was the minister, he didn't have a vote. So it was voted and passed unanimously: Nobody can be a member of this church unless they own property in the county.

Years later, Fred Craddock and his wife returned to that area. They actually had a hard time finding the church because of a new interstate highway. But finally they found the little road that led up to his former church and suddenly there it was sitting in the pine trees, beautiful and pristine. As they drove up in the church parking lot, the place was crowded with trucks and cars everywhere. Fred Craddock said: "My goodness, they must be having a revival or something." Then he saw it, a sign stuck on the front of the church which said: "Bar-B-Q, All You Can Eat $4.99."

They went inside and the place was full of folks. The pews had been pushed back against the walls, formica tables and chairs were set up, the little organ was still there over in the corner, but it had dishes stacked on it. Suddenly, it dawned on Fred Craddock what had happened. The church had died, closed down, sold out, and had become a restaurant. As Fred Craddock recalls the story, he says: "There were some of the most gosh-awful looking people in there that you've ever seen. Motorcycles out front and pickup trucks...you've never seen such a crowd. Blue-collar workers, white-collar workers. People of all ages and colors and backgrounds." Fred Craddock turned to his wife and said, "It's a good thing this place is a restaurant because if it were still the kind of church it used to be, some of these folks sure wouldn't fit in!" (Fred Craddock, *Craddock Stories,* Mike Graves and Richard Ward, eds. [St. Louis: Chalice Press, 2001], 28-9).

That day of discovery broke the heart of that former pastor. Isn't that sad? And what could be more ironic than for people who would once be denied the Bread of Life in that place being invited later to come and have "all the Bar-B-Q you can eat!"

As we read the Great Commission, it is clear that Jesus did not say: "Go therefore and make disciples of *most* of the nations, baptizing *some* of them in the name of the Father, the Son and the Holy Spirit." It says "*all* nations." The good news is intended for all people and when the Holy Spirit is in us, we will reach out and offer Christ to all people. That's number one—the Holy Spirit unites people; it brings people together and makes them one.

II. The Story Reminds Us That the Holy Spirit Excites People and That We Should Live in That Exciting Spirit

The day began in fear and frustration and boredom and ended in great excitement. The disciples felt un-qualified for the task that lay before them. Their minds were confused. Their confidence was shaken. Their nerves were jangled. Their strength was sapped. Their energy was depleted. Their hearts were empty. Their spirits were down.

Over the preceding few weeks, they had been on an unbelievable emotional roller coaster, with its incredible ups and downs. Just think of it—there was the triumphal entry into Jerusalem on Palm Sunday that was exhilarating and glorious. But that was quickly followed by the arrest of Jesus; then the trial and the conviction. They had not counted on that. It wasn't in their game plan. It shook them. It scared the life out of them. As if that weren't enough, next came Good Friday and the crucifixion. That was the toughest blow of all. Their hopes were dashed, their dreams destroyed, their spirits crushed. But then came Easter Morning! Their Lord was resurrected, and their spirits were resurrected too. They were ready now to take on the world.

But then came another jolt! Jesus told them, "I can't stay with you. I must go to My Father, and I want you to now take up this ministry of love. I want you to do it now! I want you to be the church! I want you to teach the world this message of love and sacrifice and commitment and grace and salvation! I want you to be my witnesses to all the world!" "But Lord," they protested, "we can't do that. We don't have the strength. We don't have the resources. We don't have the know-how or the power or the courage." "Don't worry," the Master promised them, "I won't leave you alone. I will send you a helper. We will pool our resources. We'll put it all together. You just bring what you have and I'll do the rest. I will send you strength and power. I will send the Holy Spirit to be with you always!" And then Jesus ascended into Heaven. And the disciples (per his instructions) waited for the gift of the Holy Spirit.

Picture this in your mind: their Lord has gone. The task is squarely on their shoulders. They feel so inadequate and so scared, and now they have to sit and wait for the Holy Spirit to come. Like us, they were not very good at waiting! On earlier occasions when Jesus told them to wait, they either, in their impatience, did the wrong thing, or in their apathy, fell asleep. Now here they are waiting, and I can just imagine the conversation in the Upper Room, a conversation filled with grumbling and griping and complaining.

"How long do we have to wait around here? This waiting is driving me up the wall." "We don't know anything about this Holy Spirit. I've never seen any Holy Spirit. I mean, how do we know it really exists?" "Maybe we misunderstood Him. We've been here a long time and nothing has happened. Maybe no Holy Spirit is coming." "Maybe it's over. Maybe we should just face up to that and accept it and go on back to our old lives." "No!" says Simon Peter. "We wait! He promised us the Holy Spirit will come and I believe him. With all my heart, I believe him."

And just at that moment, they heard something—a strange sound, away off in the distance, becoming louder and louder as it moved toward them—a sound like the rush of a mighty wind—and it blew on that place! (Oh my, did it blow on that place!) And they were all filled with the Holy Spirit, *and* they were filled with great excitement. They received courage and confidence and strength and new life. Through the power and presence and inspiration of the Holy Spirit they said yes to life, and they became the excited church of the living God on that day of Pentecost. Through the gift of the Holy Spirit they were empowered to take up the preaching, teaching, healing, caring ministry of Jesus Christ. Simon Peter stood up to preach, and when he finished, three thousand people joined the church—three thousand people from different nations, of different colors, with different backgrounds became one. They became the church.

In this powerful story, we discover the good news of our faith, namely this: We are not alone! God is with us! We can pool our resources with God, and God's strength will see us through. God will take our little and make it much. It will carry us; it will save us. Because of Pentecost, because of the gift of the Holy Spirit, because of God's sustaining presence with us, as Christian people we can face the future with steady eyes and hopeful hearts. Even when things sometimes look bleak and dreary and scary, we can live with courage and confidence and grace because God is with us.

If that doesn't excite you, then we better go get a spiritual stethoscope and check your faith heartbeat. God forgive us if we ever make the gospel boring and routine, because God is with us and God loves us and God can save us. That is the most exciting news this world has ever heard. The Holy Spirit unites us and the Holy Spirit excites us.

III. The Story Reminds Us That the Holy Spirit Invites Us and That We Should Live in That Inviting Spirit

One of the greatest lessons I ever learned about evangelism came from a business executive. This corporate consultant had been brought in to lead a workshop for the church. In the workshop, someone asked the question: "How do we get people to join the church?" The consultant started casually talking about that, and then he called me up out of the audience and said he had been standing for a long time and could he put his arm around my shoulder for support.

He talked a little more and then called another minister up and said: "I'm feeling tired. Could I put my other arm around your shoulder for support?" He talked some more and then called another minister and asked him to hold his leg and then another minister to hold his other leg. Then he called a layman up and asked him if he would stand behind him and put his arms around his waist and hold him up. He talked a bit more and then suddenly he stopped and said to the audience: "Now, forget everything I've said and tell me what you see happening up here." Silence. "Come on, now," he said, "What do you see happening up here?"

Finally someone said: "We see four ministers and one layman holding you up off the floor while you talk." "That's right," he said. "Now, isn't that amazing? How did I get them to do that?" Silence for a moment and then timidly someone said: "You asked them?" "That's right," he said, "and that's how you get people to do things. That's how you get people to join the church. You ask them!" "Now," he said, "that takes care of that. Let's move on to the next question."

That workshop haunted me because at the time I was in charge of evangelism for my church, and every week I would think of things I wanted to do and needed to do and preferred to do rather than call people and ask them to join our church. And then I would remember that corporate consultant and how he said, "If you want to get people to join the church, you've got to ask them, you've got to invite them!" There are a few people in the world who will move to town and call up and say:

"I'm here and I'd like to join your church," but they are very, very few in number. Most folks wait to be asked, want to be asked, because they want to be sure that they are wanted and welcome here.

Now let me ask you something: how many people have you asked to join your church in the past week? Oh, really? You haven't? Well, how about the past month? How about so far this year? Well, let me ask you this: In your lifetime as a Christian, how many people have you asked? How many people have you invited to come and join your church family? That's your job and mine as vessels of the Holy Spirit, to share with people our Christ and our church! It's the highest compliment you can pay somebody, to say to them: "I want to share my Savior and my church with you."

On that First Pentecost Day, the Holy Spirit blew into the heart of Simon Peter and he asked, he invited, and three thousand people came forward. The Holy Spirit unites, excites, and invites. When the wind of the Holy Spirit breathes in our hearts, we will become a part of that ministry; we will become the instruments of the Holy Spirit to unite people, excite people, and invite people to Christ and his church.

A Biblical Perspective

According to Acts 2, the Holy Spirit caused quite a stir when it arrived on the Day of Pentecost. A violent wind, tongues of fire, people talking in newly acquired languages, astonished bystanders, and even a sermon to top it off—all by 9:00 in the morning. Then those three thousand converts—it must have taken the rest of the day to baptize them. All in all, an impressive showing for the Holy Spirit.

But that was just the beginning. The rest of the book of Acts continues the story of the disruptive and transforming impact of the Holy Spirit, made operative in the world through the activities of those first apostles. Let's take a look at what happened when two of those apostles—Peter and Paul—became the conduit for the Spirit's uniting, exciting, and inviting power.

Peter and Cornelius

Scholars of the New Testament readily point out that the events described in Acts 10–11 mark a major turning point in the missional history of the early church. What did "to the ends of the earth" really mean? The story of Peter's meeting with the Roman centurion, Cornelius, is like finely stylized drama. The text shifts like a camera lens between Cornelius and Peter, highlighting once again the powerful workings of the Holy Spirit aimed at getting the word about Jesus spread as far and wide as possible. First we see Cornelius, an apparently God-fearing Gentile, startled by an angel's visitation and a strange command to find a Jew named "Simon who is called Peter." Then we see Peter, stomach growling with hunger, entranced in prayer on a hot rooftop at noon. Not surprising, he sees a vision of his own. Only what Peter sees is no angel, but an unbelievable array of unclean and clean animals, all on a big sheet; and with this vision comes the command to sit down and eat—any of it. Peter, a devout Jew, is shocked. A Jew eat a lizard or a pig? You must be kidding. Even hearing the command three times leaves Peter "greatly puzzled." Then the scene shifts back to Cornelius, who suddenly appears at Peter's gate. Imagine Peter's reaction when he hears the Holy Spirit insist that he answer the door and—of all the outrageous acts—invite a Gentile into a Jewish home to share a meal and to stay the night. It wasn't even Peter's house. You must be kidding.

The situation gets even more complicated. Cornelius invites Peter back to his house—a Jew in a Gentile home. Now Peter is confronted with the prospect of violating Torah. No observant (clean) Jew could enter a non-Jewish (unclean) household. Nonetheless, "the next day [Peter] got up and went with them." The remainder of the story concerns Peter's eventual acceptance of a mandate from the Lord to preach the gospel of Jesus to those not just outside of Jerusalem but also outside of Israel—to the Gentiles. "I truly understand that God shows no partiality" (10:34), admits Peter, and with that statement, the church is on its way to the ends of the earth. The Holy Spirit falls upon Cornelius and all in earshot of Peter, and they are all baptized, to the absolute astonishment of "the circumcised believers who had come with Peter" (10:45).

Cornelius invites Peter to stay a few days longer, and we wonder what kind of food this Peter and Cornelius shared around the dinner table. At the invitation of the Holy Spirit, Jew and Gentile had come together. And after Peter's report of this miracle to church leaders in Jerusalem (followed by some tense debate), the pronouncement was made: "So then, God has granted even the Gentiles repentance unto life" (11:18 NIV).

Paul and the Ephesian Silversmiths

The good news caused such excitement and prompted such a response that the early church could no longer be contained geographically or ethnically.

Soon Paul, the chief evangelist to the Gentiles, would be proclaiming the unity of the body of Christ throughout Asia Minor and as far as Rome. And in the meantime, in chapter after chapter of Acts, the Holy Spirit moves like a gale-force wind, breaking apostles out of prison cells, energizing debates among church leaders, empowering sermons met with stones and protest, assisting in the planting of Christian churches, and giving courage to the teams of missionaries traveling from place to place with the gospel.

Then comes the story in Acts 19 of Paul in Ephesus. He's been preaching and teaching there for two years, "so that all the residents of Asia, both Jews and Greeks, heard the word of the Lord" (19:10). He's so in tune with the Spirit's power that his very skin becomes a vehicle for people's healing. Touch a cloth that has touched Paul and your disease will be gone. Paul is at the height of his effectiveness as an evangelist—which on occasion brings him into conflict with the powers that be.

In Paul's day, Ephesus was a thriving port city, one of the commercial hubs of the ancient world. Its main attraction was the magnificent Temple of Artemis. Merchants and artisans of all kinds could make good money in Ephesus in support of the Temple activities. The power Paul possessed belonged to the Holy Spirit and when Paul one-ups the magicians, inspiring them to make a very expensive bonfire with their spell books, he hits the economic nerve of the city. The local metalworkers (they make silver pieces for the worship of Artemis) rise up in protest. Demetrius, the spokesperson, gathers a crowd of supporters to challenge Paul. He works them up into a frenzy over the economic danger posed by a message that undermines idolatry and thus the industry that depends on it. A riot ensues; some of Paul's companions are dragged off to the great amphitheater; the angry mob chants, "Great is Artemis" until their voices give out. Finally a city official makes a plea for sanity: a riot could bring the Roman soldiers. The people disperse.

Paul leaves Ephesus soon after that; yet his confrontation with the Ephesians highlights the real risks that accompany the Holy Spirit's activity in the world. The Spirit's work through Paul for those two years threatened to transform an entire city. In truth, the gospel has the potential to challenge the assumptions and shake the structures of any culture. The Spirit's work challenged the disciples to go to those who worshiped differently (despised Samaritans), then to those who looked different (an Ethiopian), and then to those who lived differently (the pagan Ephesians). When the Spirit uses us, we are liable to cause no little disturbance in our world.

We can trust God to provide us with the resources to do God's work and ministry. We may have limited resources, vision, and capacity, but God can take our limitations and help us transform the world.

(See *Wesley Study Bible*, Life Application Topic: *Go and Tell*, p. 1205, and Wesleyan Core Term: *World as Parish*, p. 1322.)

Session Six

God Takes Mere Sinners and Makes Us *More* than Conquerors

ROMANS 8:28-39

Her name was Julia. She was stricken with cancer when she was sixteen years old. During the next three years, she and her family made over forty trips to the Houston Medical Center. There was a lot of pain, a lot of discomfort, a lot of broken dreams, a lot of disappointments, but through it all, Julia never lost her faith. She never lost her smile. She never lost her sense of humor. Sadly, she died—just nineteen years old! Just before she passed away, I went again to see her. She said something to me that I will never forget. She realized that her time on this earth was short, and she said, "Jim, for three years now, you and others have prayed and prayed that I might be made well, that I won't have to suffer anymore." She smiled, took my hand, and said, "Soon now, your prayers will be answered. I'm gonna be made well. The suffering will be over and I'll be with

God! I'll miss my family and my friends, but I'll be with God and I will be well!"

Some would say cancer defeated her, but it didn't. It didn't because her indomitable Christian spirit made her not just a victim but a victor. At her funeral, when I read this Romans 8 passage, I accidentally put the emphasis on the word *more* and the text took on a fresh meaning, especially as I reflected on Julia's life. We are *more* than conquerors! We can't always win in this world, but we can, with the help of God, always be more than conquerors. The message of our Christian faith is that with the spirit of Christ we can be victors even when we are victims.

Have you heard about the young man who wanted a job as an usher in a movie house? The owner was interviewing the young man to see if he could handle the usher job, and he asked him, "Son, what would you do if the theater caught on fire?" The young man answered, "Well, sir, you don't have to worry about me. I'd be the first one out of here!"

That was not the answer the owner was hoping for, because, you see, that's not enough! The young man would have conquered the situation and saved his own skin, but as an usher *more* would be expected of him than that.

Remember the temptation experience of Jesus in the wilderness? He had gone there early on to meditate and pray and think through the kind of ministry he should have. There in the wilderness, Jesus was tempted in three different ways to become a conqueror. He was tempted to become a powerful economic liberator, a victorious military leader, and a magical wonder-worker, but he resisted all of those temptations and chose instead the way of love, the way of the cross, the way of the Suffering Servant. Jesus refused to overpower or overwhelm or coerce people with brute force. You see, Jesus chose to be more than a conqueror.

Remember the rich young ruler? He was a conqueror. He had won out in the financial world, in the world of success, leadership, power. He had clout! He was a rich, young ruler, a conqueror. But look! It is not enough. There was something lacking in his life. Wealth, youth, and power were not enough! Winning was not enough. There was a vacuum, a hunger, an emptiness. Jesus saw it and said to him: "Follow me and I'll give you something more fulfilling. Follow me and I will make you more than a conqueror!"

Christ is trying to tell us something very important. Christ is showing us, as a baby in a manger and as a Savior on a cross, that the happy people, the fulfilled people, the genuine people are not bullies, not the power mongers, not the selfish people, not the mean-spirited people. Christ is calling us to be "more than conquerors," to be merciful, humble, and thoughtful, to be considerate, patient and kind, forgiving and loving. Of course, there are times when we have to defend ourselves and others, but basically Christ is teaching us to walk through life gently and graciously so that we don't selfishly elbow other people out of our way or push or shove or grab or possess.

Let me hurry to say that this doesn't mean weakness; it means strength—the strength of bigness and love, the magnanimity and courage to choose to be more than conquerors! Now let me be more specific and bring this a little closer to our daily lives.

I. As Christians, We Are Called to Be More than Conquerors in the Home with Our Children

Some parents approach parenthood as "conquerors." They see their children as things to be conquered or as problems to be controlled rather than as persons to be loved.

Sometimes in the counseling room, I hear children and young people exclaim, "If just once my parents would say 'thank you' or 'please' to me, I would feel more like a human being. If only they would treat me like a person with feelings."

Some years ago, when our son, Jeff, was born, I can remember standing in the corridor of the hospital one night looking in the nursery window, with my nose pressed against the glass, admiring our new little boy. A lady came over and said, "Is that your baby?" I proudly answered, "Yes!" And then she said, "Isn't that something . . . he looks just like a little person!" I thought to myself, "He is! That's exactly what he is, a little person." But sometimes we parents forget that, don't we? We forget that children are persons, and we give way to the temptation to treat them as things to be conquered.

Recently I was having lunch with a friend of mine who happens to be a child psychologist. At the next table there was a young woman who was having a terrible time with her daughter, a young preschooler who looked to be about three years old. They had obviously been shopping and the little girl was tired and sleepy. She spilled her water and she dropped her spoon and she got some food on her dress. The mother was scolding her and jerking her impatiently and slapping at her and talking to her in a very hostile tone, calling her "stupid."

As we left the restaurant, that mother and daughter were standing by the door and my friend stopped. He felt so sorry for the little girl that he knelt down in front of her and said to her, "You know, you are a very special little girl and I like you!" He patted her on the shoulder and she smiled. As he stood up, the mother wasn't smiling! She cut her eyes toward him and said, "You don't approve, do you?" My friend looked at the woman and said, "Well, it's just that I'm a psychologist and I know what you are doing to this child!"

Now let me ask you something. What are we doing to our children? How do we treat them? How do we relate to them? How do we view them? As things to be conquered or as persons to be loved? Please don't misunderstand me. I am all for good, loving discipline. It's one of the best ways to express love and give children security. But I'm talking here about attitudes—and I simply want to remind us that as Christians, we are called to be more than conquerors with our children.

Of course, this can be turned around. Some children and youth are guilty here too. They forget that parents are people. Some children and youth view their parents as things to be conquered or outwitted or tricked, and that's just as bad. Christian love means being "more than conquerors" in the home.

II. Second, as Christians We Are Called to Be More than Conquerors with Our Mates (Or If You Are Not Married, Your "Dates")

It has always bothered me on the college campus or in the high school corridor or in the business office to hear men talk about their sexual conquests. The word "conquest" is a revealing word, isn't it? The very word "conquest" sounds sacrilegious because it arrogantly refers to another human being as a kind of sexual object, an accessory, a plaything to be conquered, used, and discarded. There is something very un-Christian about that!

Just as wrong is the beautiful high school or college girl or career woman who holds her man on a string and displays him like a fisherman showing off a prize catch—catching and conquering—breaking hearts along the way. It's wrong because we are called to be *more* than conquerors.

Then there are many couples who spend their entire married life in competition with each other—vying for power and position, trying to get the upper hand, each partner trying to conquer the other.

Once a couple came to see me. They had been married less than a month and were already having a harsh disagreement. I took him aside and said, "Look, Tom, it's not worth it. For the sake of your marriage, why not give in?" He said, "Oh, no! I can't do that! I can't let her get the upper hand in this, or I'll be henpecked!" Then I took her aside and asked her if she could give in for the sake of the marriage, and she answered, "Oh, no! If I let him have his way in this, he will take control and boss me around for the rest of our days!" Their marriage lasted about six months because they didn't understand how to be more than conquerors with their mate.

III. Finally, as Christians We Are Called to Be More than Conquerors with God

Some people try to conquer God. They want to put God in their pocket like a rabbit's foot. Some of us want

God to be like a genie in a bottle where we can control him and keep him safely tucked away till we need him, and then we let him out to do us a special favor. Some try to master God and make him their ever-ready servant, rather than their sovereign Lord. But, you see, this misses the point. We can't conquer God. History documents that, over and over. He won't be defeated. When he was a baby, they tried to kill him. When he became a man, they tried to kill him. But God's truth can't be killed. It resurrects! It lives on! It endures! Even when he was a victim, he became a victor.

One of the most beloved legends of Christmas is the Little Drummer Boy. When the Christ Child was born, many beautiful gifts were brought to the manger, so the story goes. Gifts of great beauty and splendor. But one small boy was very poor. He had nothing to offer the Lord and this made him very sad. Then he thought, "I can play my drum for him." And so he did. *Pa-rum-pum-pum-pum. Pa-rum-pum-pum-pum.* He played with all the love in his heart, and as he played, according to the legend, the Christ Child smiled, showing that the gift of love is the best gift of all!

So, if you want to bring a smile to the face of Christ, don't go through life beating up on people but rather beat the drum of love. Go out into all the world—in God's Spirit—and be more than a conqueror!

A Biblical Perspective

The tone of Paul's series of questions in Romans 8:31-39 is confident and celebratory. Paul's aim is to leave no doubt that if God is on our side, then nothing in this world can ever come between us. Even before the battle has begun, we are already "more than conquerors." God has given us Christ, in effect, promising to give us everything we need through that greatest gift of all. And nothing on earth or in heaven can take that away.

> No creation, not even time or space, can ever separate the Creator from those whom he loves.... No creaturely power—the only other power than God's, since there are no other gods—can affect our lives in any but a temporary way....
>
> Perhaps the greatest comfort here lies in the fact that we too are creatures. If no creature can separate us from God's love, then in the end even our own almost limitless ability to rebel against God is overcome; and we are saved from our last greatest enemy, ourselves. God has known us from the first and set us on the path of a destiny surrounded by his love. (Paul Achtemeier, *Romans* [Atlanta: John Knox Press, 1985], 150)

This almost sounds too good to be true. And yet, what would it mean for us to live fully in the assurance of God's unconditional, sustaining, all-encompassing love? What about all those times we have stumbled in our faith, fallen into sin, turned and walked away, or followed other gods? What about all the forces at work in our world, bent on making us self-absorbed consumers, or stressed-out workaholics, or moral relativists? Don't we have to measure up to some standard, follow a set of rules, perform a certain number of good deeds, or stay within a specified boundary?

According to Paul, no. So can we be assured our salvation is truly a gift from God, not a reward for good behavior? Those of us reading Romans today may be inclined to take Paul's conclusions for granted. They hardly seem surprising anymore. Yet in the history of Christianity, Romans proved to be radically transforming, especially for several influential figures who, after encountering Paul's arguments, became more than conquerors themselves, surmounting obstacles of every kind to change or shape our church even today.

Augustine

Augustine's father was a nonbeliever and his mother was a devout Christian. And by the time Augustine was born (A.D. 354) in North Africa in what is now eastern Algeria, the scattered enclaves of Christian communities that Paul and the first apostles had founded had grown into an institutionalized church—no longer under persecution—sanctioned by the Roman emperor. But now it was being shaped by controversies, councils of bishops, and political instability and intrigue.

At an early age, Augustine showed signs of possessing exceptional intellectual abilities. He was sent to study rhetoric, which was the study of the technique and rules for using language effectively, especially in public speaking. Eventually he became a teacher of rhetoric in Milan, Italy, where he met many people, including the famous Bishop Ambrose. But although he was a teacher, Augustine remained an earnest student, seeking the truth in various philosophies and, all the while, struggling to shake what he knew about the Christian faith.

One day, as Augustine was sitting in a garden, he heard the voice of child sing out, "Take up and read, take up and read." Believing the voice to be divine direction, Augustine took up Paul's letter to the Romans and read 13:13-14: "Let us live honorably as in the day, not in reveling and drunkenness, not in debauchery and licentiousness, not in quarreling and jealousy. Instead, put on the Lord Jesus Christ, and make no provision for the flesh, to gratify its desires." Augustine gave up his lifestyle (including his concubine) and his teaching job and moved to Cassiciacum (near Milan) to devote himself to a monastic life of study and contemplation. Eventually, as he became more and more well known, he was asked to become Bishop of Hippo, which was close to where he was born. As an ordained member of the episcopy, Augustine devoted his great intellect and pastoral energies to preaching the Scriptures, writing commentaries, opposing the prevailing heresies of the day (Manicheism, Donatism, and Pelagianism), and explaining the doctrines of the Church. Besides Jesus, the Disciples, and the Apostle Paul, no other person has so influenced the way we think about who we are as Christians. His writings were widely read and quoted throughout the history of the Catholic Church as well as by the Protestant reformers of the sixteenth century. Even today when students take their first theology course, they are introduced to the writings of Augustine.

More than a conqueror, Augustine overcame the lure of lust, pride, and vanity to become a key defender and interpreter of the Christian faith during a critical time— a remarkable journey that began in an Italian garden with a Bible open to the book of Romans.

Luther

Another giant in the array of Christian theologians is Martin Luther, one of the foremost leaders of the

Protestant Reformation in Europe. While many aspects of his legacy are still debated, Catholic and Protestant scholars agree that Luther emerged on the scene at a most opportune moment, with the necessary conviction and courage to pursue a plan of action that altered the course of the Church.

At the beginning of the sixteenth century, the Roman Catholic Church was in grave trouble. Corruption, immorality, and political shenanigans had become commonplace at every level of the Church, from the pope down to the local priest and nun. It was into this environment that Luther came of age.

After a strict upbringing and an equally severe university experience, Luther left behind his legal studies to enter the Augustinian monastery at Erfurt, Germany. His hope was that a disciplined monastic life would justify or make him right with God and assure him of his salvation. It did not. In spite of his rigorous daily regimen of meditation, study, and prayer, and years of lecturing on the Bible, Luther was terrified of God's justice, certain that his overwhelming sinfulness would consign him to hell.

Then, at some point in his struggle to make sense of his anguish, Luther reread the opening chapter of Romans: "The one who is righteous will live by faith" (1:17). This time he heard new meaning and at last his mortal dread was relieved. Luther came to see God's righteousness not as an unattainable standard against which sinners are judged and condemned but as God's gift freely given and received by faith. Luther experienced God's grace.

Luther's newly discovered perspective freed him from personal despair, but it also set him on a collision course with the leaders of the Roman Catholic Church. By now the Church was an expert practiced in making money on the penance of its sinners. In the early sixteenth century, Pope Leo X authorized the sale of indulgences: for a fee, a sinner could buy a document assuring him or her (or a departed loved one) a shorter stay in purgatory, the halfway house between heaven and hell, where people suffered until they were fortunate enough to earn their way to heaven. Luther, now assured of his own salvation because he was saved by grace alone, took a stand against the Church's attempt to offer such assurance of its own authority.

Luther wrote out his list of grievances against the Church, and nailed it to the Wittenberg castle door. He also had the grievances published and disseminated throughout Germany, and the rest of Europe quickly followed. Luther's 95 Theses became a lightning rod both for supporters of church reform all over Europe and for the defenders of the status quo. He was reviled and praised. Remarkably, Luther's action, as risky as it was, did not get him burned at the stake as were so many others. Instead, he is still known to the world as the monk who defied the pope and emperor in the name of Scripture.

Wesley

After her five-year-old son, John, was pulled from a burning house, Susanna Wesley was convinced God had big plans for his future. She was right. John Wesley set into motion a reform movement within his own Anglican tradition that became one of the largest Protestant denominations in the world.

At Oxford University in Oxford, England, John Wesley was a bright scholar and a devout Christian, eventually joining a covenant group of like-minded friends (including his brother Charles), committed to leading a holy life and to holding one another accountable for how they practiced that life.

For a while, that brand of piety seemed sufficient for Wesley. Then in 1735, Wesley joined a group of Moravian missionaries bound for the New World. He planned to preach to the Native Americans. Wesley had accepted an invitation from the governor of Georgia to serve a local parish in Savannah. His tenure as a pastor, however, was brief and ineffective, full of disaster. Wesley returned to England disillusioned; moreover, his experience in America troubled him. Like Augustine and Luther before him, Wesley began to question his own salvation. Others, like the Moravians, seemed so confident. He, on the other hand, suffered with doubt and anxiety. How could God be so present to others and so far from him?

Then something happened. One May evening, at his brother's invitation, Wesley attended a Moravian society meeting held on Aldersgate Street in London. Here he listened to a reading from Martin Luther's preface to the book of Romans. In his journal, he recalls feeling his heart "strangely warmed" and becoming suddenly aware that he did trust Christ for his salvation: "An assurance was given to me, that he had taken away *my* sin, even *mine*, and saved *me* from the law of sin and death" (*Journal*, May 24, 1738).

No longer in doubt of his own salvation, Wesley went to work preaching salvation to others, particularly to those often neglected by his fellow Anglican clergymen—the poor and marginalized who inhabited the urban centers of the burgeoning Industrial Revolution.

Wesley rode thousands of miles on horseback to preach thousands of sermons to thousands of people. Along the way, he established small groups as a means of holding people accountable for their personal piety, and created an army of lay preachers to help share the gospel as widely as possible. Once a young priest unsure of his own faith, John Wesley became a leader of a great revival, the founder of a religious movement, a prolific writer of religious materials, and the exemplar of social holiness.

(See *Wesley Study Bible*, Life Application Topic: *Spiritual Gifts*, p. 1368; and Wesleyan Core Terms: *Law Established through Faith*, p. 1371; *Justification*, p. 1373, *Power of Sin*, p. 1374; and *Spirit of Bondage*, p. 1377.)

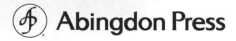